THE PRINCIPLE OF
MANIFESTATION

A Practical Guide to How We Materialize the Physical Universe

RUSSELL ANTHONY GIBBS

Copyright © 2018 Russell Anthony Gibbs.

All rights reserved. No part of this book may be reproduced, stored, or transmitted by any means—whether auditory, graphic, mechanical, or electronic—without written permission of the author, except in the case of brief excerpts used in critical articles and reviews. Unauthorized reproduction of any part of this work is illegal and is punishable by law.

ISBN: 978-1-7320521-0-9 (paperback)
ISBN: 978-1-7320521-1-6 (hardback)
ISBN: 978-1-7320521-2-3 (eBook)

Rev. date: 4/25/2018

Contents

Introduction 1
Important Definitions 3

The Principle of Manifestation 11
1. Defining the Principle of Manifestation 11
    Scientific References of Manifestation 13
    Religious References of Manifestation 15
    Metaphysical References of Manifestation 18
    New Thought References of Manifestation 19
    New Age References of Manifestation 21
    Summary of References of Manifestation 22

2. The Mechanics of Manifestation 25
    Components of Deliberate Manifestation 27
    A. Alignment of Consciousness................................28
    B. Desire Deliberately..35
    C. Believe and Allow Manifestation 38
    Summary of the Mechanics of Manifestation 40

3. Living the Principle of Manifestation 43
    A. Achieving Consciousness Alignment 44
    B. Desire Deliberately..61
    C. Believe and Allow Manifestation 78
    Summary of Living the Principle of Manifestation 85

Special Message to the Reader 89
About the Author 91
Acknowledgments 93
Index of Quoted Authors...95

Introduction

The Principle of Manifestation is the third book in a series of eight books on enlightenment. The first book, *The Six Principles of Enlightenment and Meaning of Life*, is an intellectual and spiritual overview of the six enlightenment principles that explain the nature of our existence. This book, ***The Principle of Manifestation***, expands on the second principle and explains how we manifest the physical reality through our consciousness. The process of manifestation is not a new concept and has been discussed and written about for thousands of years. To support the explanation of manifestation, I have incorporated quotes from enlightened beings, scientists, spiritual leaders, artists, philosophers and other insightful individuals. If you are unfamiliar with any of the quoted authors in this book, please reference the Index of Quoted Authors in the back. Additionally, I have provided practical methods and practices to live and experience the Principle of Manifestation. This book is intended to be a stand-alone work; however, the other five principles of the series are referenced when necessary to illuminate the Principle of Manifestation.

These are the six principles of enlightenment:

The Principle of Oneness
The Principle of Manifestation
The Principle of Multiple Realities
The Principle of Timelessness
The Principle of Neutrality and Nonjudgment
The Principle of Openness

The goal of this book is to help the reader understand and master the manifestation process. The power of mind over matter is extremely beneficial in our daily existence. When we master manifestation, we have the ability to create the life of our dreams. Good luck on your journey to understanding this principle.

Important Definitions

THERE ARE SEVERAL TERMS AND concepts used in this book that are worth clarifying at the beginning. Here is a short list of some key terms and concepts used to explain the Principle of Manifestation.

Quantum Mechanics

Also referred to as quantum physics or quantum field theory, **quantum mechanics** is a branch of study that explains the behavior of matter and energy on the molecular, atomic and subatomic levels. Quantum mechanics deals with the laws governing the very small pieces of matter and energy that make up everything in the universe. The universe is a quantum field of energy and matter. This quantum field is constantly transforming from energy to matter, then back to energy again. When matter is broken down or energy is collided, the other is created. This cycle is fundamental to the Principle of Manifestation. Everything physical and non-physical is a form of energy. Physical matter is merely slower vibrating energy that is visible to the human senses.

The more you understand the theories of quantum mechanics, the stranger they seem. On the atomic and subatomic levels, matter and energy behave entirely differently from what we see on a bigger scale in the physical world. On a large scale, the world appears as a variety of objects that can be solid, liquid, plasma or gas. On an atomic level, there appears to be nothing solid and 99.99 percent empty space (atomic emptiness); the remainder is moving quickly and phasing in and out, with no exact position in space. On an atomic level, everything is moving in a constant state of flux with indeterminate positions. Again, none of this matches up with the solid, stable, physical world we perceive and experience in our ordinary reality.

Vibrational Frequency

All energy and matter is moving and vibrating at its core. String theory, from quantum mechanics, explains that all energy and matter at its subatomic core can be reduced to a miniscule, string-like, vibrating filament. This string-like filament is identical in everything but its vibrational frequency determines what it appears as in the physical reality. The different vibrational frequencies determine if something manifests as water, soil, air or a human cell.

Consciousness (Awareness)

The concept of consciousness has perplexed philosophers and scientists alike for centuries. Consciousness can be defined as a state or quality of awareness. It can also be described as the source of all cognitive processes, from which thoughts, beliefs and emotions originate. There are various theories about where consciousness is located. Some scientists and philosophers believe consciousness (or the mind) is nonphysical and separate of the physical being (dualism), others think it could be contained in the brain as a neural activity (materialism). Classical philosophers, such as Plato and Aristotle, connected consciousness to the concept of the soul or spirit and were dualist in their thinking.

One additional view about consciousness, known as panpsychism, is that everything material—even down to the subatomic level—has individual consciousness. This means everything has a degree or type of consciousness, including plants, soil, air, water and even man-made structures. Panpsychism is one of the oldest philosophical theories about consciousness and can be found in the teachings of Vedanta, Mahayana Buddhism, Shinto, Taoism, Paganism, Shamanism, Plato, Aristotle, Baruch Spinoza and Charles Darwin. I ascribe to the concept of panpsychism and believe that a shared collective consciousness is the conduit that unifies the Universe.

Levels of Consciousness (Awareness)

The renowned psychologist Carl Jung and neurologist Sigmund Freud further theorized that consciousness has at least three different level of awareness. Although their levels differ in name and type, they add a complexity and depth to consciousness. Both Jung and Freud believed that most of our consciousness is not easily accessible and that the small part that is, can be compared with the tip of an iceberg. Jung's deepest layer of consciousness, the collective unconscious, is the level shared by beings of the same species.

I believe that there are possibly many more than three levels to consciousness and that on the deepest level there is shared collective consciousness of the entire Universe—not only humans but animals, plants and anything material down to a subatomic level. There could be personal and group consciousness based upon gender, nationality, ethnicity or anything a person chooses to identify with. Then there are several levels of less accessible subconsciousness—both personal and group—and additional levels of unconsciousness that are personal, group and collective. All these levels of connected consciousness add to the complexity of the collective consciousness of the entire Universe. In religious terms, the highest level of collective consciousness is synonymous with God or the Divine. In quantum mechanics, the highest level of collective consciousness is synonymous with the infinite quantum energy field.

Emotions

Emotions are complex and can be described as instinctive states or intuitive feelings derived from one's circumstances. Scientists have not come to a consensus on what actually triggers emotions or their function. There are three types of theories that emotions, however, could be triggered physiologically, neurologically or cognitively. That is, emotions could be triggered by your physical body, your brain activities or your thought processes. I believe that emotions could be triggered by all three but are primarily a product of our cognitive processes.

Among other things, emotions tell us how we are thinking. Emotions signal consistency or conflict with our thoughts and beliefs among the various levels of consciousness. Positive emotions feel good and signal consistent thoughts and beliefs in the conscious, subconscious and unconscious levels. Negative emotions feel unpleasant and signal conflicting thoughts and beliefs in the various level of consciousness. Emotions are efficient signals of our thoughts and beliefs, and are a shortcut to doing deep analysis of our cognitive process. Emotions also reveal whether the thoughts in our personal consciousness are consistent and in agreement with the higher collective consciousness. Positive emotions signal consciousness alignment and negative emotions signal misalignment of consciousness.

The Universe, God and "all that is"

The Universe, or God, describes the infinite essence that encompasses "all that is." Much is unknown or misinterpreted regarding the nature of the Universe/God. There has been some speculation that the human mind may not be capable of comprehending the enormity of the concept. Regardless of our human mental capacity, we are by definition part of "all that is" and consequently part of the Universe/God. God has also been called your higher self. God is actually the highest level of collective consciousness and also known as the quantum energy field from quantum mechanics. The concepts of the quantum energy field and the highest level of collective consciousness are very abstract and difficult to comprehend. For some, the notion of God or the Universe may be an easier concept to understand and experience.

Mindfulness

Mindfulness is a psychological and spiritual process that encourages present moment awareness of your thoughts, beliefs, emotions and experiences. Mindfulness is being fully present in the now. Mindfulness is important to the manifestation process because it is your stream of consciousness— accessed through your mind—that directs what you manifest in your reality. Through mindfulness, you gain awareness to what your stream of consciousness is planning to create. Mindfulness gives you the opportunity to then make changes to your thoughts, beliefs, emotions and experiences, and change what manifests in your reality.

The Principle of Manifestation

1. Defining the Principle of Manifestation

The Principle of Manifestation explains how consciousness (awareness) causes our reality to materialize. Certain activities of consciousness—such as thoughts, beliefs or even mental fixations—cause the transformation of an invisible quantum energy field into physical matter. Everything in the physical universe manifests from this source energy field. Manifestation is directed by the multiple levels of consciousness, including the subconsciousness, unconsciousness and the collective consciousness. Everything has a degree of consciousness, including animals, plants and even inanimate objects. Everyone and everything is a part of the collective consciousness and plays a role in co-creating the physical universe.

This source energy field is **"all that is"** and is also identified as the quantum energy field, the collective consciousness, the Universe and God or other names for the Divine. Much of this source energy field is invisible to human senses, and we are generally only aware of the visible physical matter. Everyone and everything is connected to this energy field, including you, other people, animals, plants, inanimate objects and even abstract concepts such as thoughts and beliefs. The source energy field, as explained in ***The Principle of Oneness***, is one, all-inclusive infinite entity that transcends both space and time. The physical part of the energy field is only a small portion (less than 5 percent) and most of the source energy field is invisible, nonphysical energy. Your personal consciousness may be unaware that other aspects of the broader collective consciousness are influencing the source energy field to manifest portions of reality. The source energy field is in a constant state of flux and is converting from nonphysical energy to physical matter and back again.

As you learn to master manifestation, you will realize that you control and manifest everything in your life. You control everything with your consciousness and access it through your mind. Your mind is not your consciousness, but your mind is a portal to access consciousness. Your personal consciousness is part of the infinite knowledge and power of the collective consciousness/source energy field. By allowing this energy to flow through you, you can manifest anything you desire.

Throughout history, the Principle of Manifestation has been referenced and explained through science, religion and philosophy. The various explanations provide a number of ways to understand the manifestation process.

Scientific References of Manifestation

Nobel Prize-winning physicist Max Planck recognized that all matter is a result of the forces of consciousness, and that this somehow causes matter to manifest. He further acknowledged that we ourselves play an essential role in the mystery of our own reality.

> There is no matter as such.
> All matter originates and exists only by virtue of a force which brings the particle of an atom to vibration and holds this most minute solar system of the atom together.
> We must assume behind this force
> the existence of a conscious and intelligent Mind.
> This Mind is the matrix of all matter.
> —Max Planck

> Science cannot solve the ultimate mystery of nature.
> And that is because, in the last analysis,
> we ourselves are a part of the mystery
> that we are trying to solve.
> —Max Planck

Albert Einstein further explained that everything, even physical matter, is a form of energy. Most energy is invisible because it is vibrating too high to see, and the physical matter we can see is just lower vibrating energy that becomes perceptible to the human senses.

> Concerning matter, we have been all wrong.
> What we have called matter is energy,
> whose vibration has been so lowered
> as to be perceptible to the senses.
> There is no matter.
> —Albert Einstein

Nikola Tesla explained that to understand the secrets of the universe, you must understand the vibrational frequencies of energy. This is consistent with Einstein's belief that the physical matter we can see is just lower vibrating energy manifesting in our reality.

> If you want to find the secrets of the universe,
> think in terms of energy, frequency and vibration.
> —Nikola Tesla

All energy and matter exists in a quantum energy field and is constantly moving and vibrating even though we may not be aware of it. Understanding and controlling the vibrational frequency of this source field of energy is a key component to mastering the manifestation process. The vibration of energy is influenced by our consciousness and other forms of consciousness that make up collective consciousness.

Religious References of Manifestation

Nearly all religions, as well as hundreds of other cultures, have a **creation myth** of how the universe and man came into existence. These creation myths are often broad, mysterious, symbolic narratives of the Principle of Manifestation on a cosmic level. Super-natural beings are usually the source of the manifestation of the universe and may or may not be credited with the ongoing manifestations of daily existence. That is why God, in his/her many names, has been identified as the creator of everything.

The question then becomes who or what is God?

God is "**all that is**," and this is synonymous with the source energy field. The physical universe is manifested from this underlying source energy field/God. We are both part of the energy field/God, and all of God is contained within our consciousness. We are often unaware of our Oneness with God/the Universe and do not realize that we are ultimately controlling all manifestation with our personal consciousness, unconsciousness and the collective consciousness. When we pray to God or ask the Universe for something, we are actually communicating with our broader, higher-self/collective consciousness. The act of prayer is focusing your thoughts/beliefs on a desire that your broader-self /God/the Universe answers and manifests. Faith and belief in God/the Universe calls forth the power of the collective consciousness to manifest in our physical reality. Whether you manifest through your personal consciousness or through God/the collective consciousness, you are always in control. Jesus attempted to explain this to his persecutors.

> The Jews took up stones again to stone him. Jesus replied,
> "I have shown you many good works from the Father.
> For which of these are you going to stone me?"
> The Jews answered,
> "It is not for a good work that we are going to stone you,
> but for blasphemy, because you, though only a human being,
> are making yourself God."
> Jesus answered, "Is it not written in your law,
> 'I said, you are gods'?
> If those to whom the word of God came were called 'gods'
> —and the scripture cannot be annulled—
> can you say that the one whom the Father has sanctified
> and sent into the world is blaspheming because I said,
> 'I am God's Son'?
> If I am not doing the works of my Father,
> then do not believe me.
> But if I do them, even though you do not believe me,
> believe the works, so that you may know and understand
> that the Father is in me and I am in the Father."

> Then they tried to arrest him again,
> but he escaped from their hands.
> —John 10:31–40 (NRSV)

Jesus says "you are gods" and that "the Father is in me and I am in the Father." This is a literal instance of Jesus explaining that we are gods and that the Divine energy force (the Father) is omnipresent within us, while we are also omnipresent within God. This reference is the same concept of everyone and everything being part of the source energy field, also known as the collective consciousness.

Other quotes attributed to Jesus reference mental agreement, asking, faith and belief as mental activities that affect reality. These are all specific acts of consciousness that cause manifestation.

> Again, truly I tell you,
> if two of you agree on earth about anything you ask,
> it will be done for you by my Father in heaven.
> —Jesus, Matthew 18:19 (NRSV)

> He said to them, "Because of your little faith.
> For truly I tell you,
> if you have faith the size of a mustard seed,
> you will say to this mountain,
> 'Move from here to there,' and it will move;
> and nothing will be impossible for you."
> —Jesus, Matthew 17:20 (NRSV)

> So I tell you, whatever you ask for in prayer,
> believe that you have received it, and it will be yours.
> —Jesus, Mark 11:24 (NRSV)

Metaphysical References of Manifestation

Metaphysics is a branch of philosophy that explores the nature of our reality, and it is discussed in several schools of Buddhism and Hinduism. Buddha conveyed clear views regarding the nature of our reality when he spoke about the mechanics of manifestation. He often emphasized the connection of thought and the resulting manifestations.

> All that we are
> is the result of what we have thought.
> The mind is everything.
> What we think we become.
> —Buddha

> We are what we think.
> All that we are arises with our thoughts.
> With our thoughts, we make the world.
> —Buddha

> Since everything is a reflection of our minds,
> everything can be changed by our minds.
> —Buddha

> The world is a looking glass.
> It gives back to every man
> a true reflection of his own thoughts.
> Rule your mind or it will rule you.
> —Buddha

> All that we are is the result of what we have thought.
> If a man speaks or acts with an evil thought,
> pain follows him.
> If a man speaks or acts with a pure thought,
> happiness follows him,
> like a shadow that never leaves him.
> —Buddha

> It is wrong to think that misfortunes
> come from the east or from the west;
> they originate within one's own mind.
> Therefore, it is foolish to guard against misfortunes
> from the external world
> and leave the inner mind uncontrolled.
> —Buddha

New Thought References of Manifestation

New Thought is a spiritual and philosophical movement that developed in the United States in the 1830s following the writing and teaching of Phineas Quimby. Psychologist and philosopher William James labeled New Thought **"the religion of healthy-mindedness"** in his study on religion and science *The Varieties of Religion Experience*. Numerous churches and groups developed around the New Thought movement, including the Unity Church, Religious Science and the Church of Divine Science.

According to the International New Thought Alliance, a key principle of New Thought is the beliefs that

> "our mental states are carried forward into manifestation and become our experience in daily living".

New Thought teachers and advocates promote the idea that the power of our thoughts, visions and words manifest our physical reality. Wallace D. Wattles also referenced the source energy field calling it the "original substance."

> Everything you see on earth
> is made from one original substance,
> out of which all things proceed.
> It is a thinking stuff from which all things are made,
> and which, in its original state, permeates, penetrates,
> and fills the inter-spaces of the universe.
> A thought, in this substance,
> produces the thing that is imaged by the thought.
> Man can form things in his thought, and,
> by impressing his thought upon formless substance,
> can cause the thing he thinks about to be created.
> —Wallace D. Wattles

> The invisible forces are ever working for man
> who is always "pulling the strings" himself,
> though he does not know it.
> Owing to the vibratory power of words,
> whatever man voices, he begins to attract.
> —Florence Scovel Shinn

> What you radiate outward in your thoughts,
> feelings, mental pictures and words,
> you attract into your life.
> —Catherine Ponder

New Age References of Manifestation

The **New Age** spiritual movement, which began in Western society during the 1970s, references manifestation with a different explanation. A predominate New Age term for the manifestation process is the **Law of Attraction**. The Law of Attraction has its roots in New Thought philosophy and is the belief that "like energies attract like energies." Positive or negative thoughts or beliefs (energies) will attract and manifest positive or negative experiences in physical reality. The Law of Attraction also emphasizes the vibrations and emotional feelings of the energies of thoughts and beliefs.

Use whatever excuse you can to vibrate in harmony
with those things you've been saying you want.
And when you do,
those things that are a vibrational equivalent
flow into your experience in abundance.
Not because you deserve it, not because you've earned it,
but because it's the natural consequence
of the Law of Attraction.
That which is like unto itself is drawn.
—Esther Hicks

I attract to my life whatever I give my attention,
energy and focus to,
whether positive or negative.
—Michael Losier

As soon as you start to feel differently
about what you already have,
you will start to attract more of the good things,
more of the things you can be grateful for.
—Joe Vitale

Summary of References of Manifestation

All the references of the Principle of Manifestation are simply attempts to explain the process of our consciousness transforming energy into matter. The physical world is manifested from an invisible source energy field. This energy field also has been known as a quantum energy field, the collective consciousness, the Universe and God or the Divine. The source energy field is omnipresent and transcends both space and time. Everything exists as potentiality within the source energy field until consciousness activities cause the energy to manifest.

Awareness or consciousness is what directs areas of the source energy field causing manifestation. A combination of your personal consciousness, unconsciousness and collective consciousness ultimately manifested your physical incarnation, including all aspects of who and what you are. The balance of the physical universe arises from the other connected individual consciousness of animate and inanimate objects that make up the collective consciousness. What we regard as inanimate substances—such as air or soil—manifest unconsciously with an innate energy to materialize. The entire physical world is self-created from the awareness of collective consciousness.

The more we understand the mechanics of manifestation the better we can use our consciousness to direct the source energy field and create the reality we wish to experience. However, not all manifestations occur deliberately. Some manifestations are caused by the subconsciousness, unconsciousness or collective consciousness. Some unconscious manifestations we like and some we do not. We can proactively achieve anything we want in this lifetime if we master deliberate manifestation.

One overriding theme of the Principle of Manifestation is that your outer world reality is a direct reflection and projection of your inner consciousness. If the outer world is turbulent, it is because your inner consciousness is turbulent. If you calm your inner self, your outer world will mirror the calm. Master your inner consciousness and you will master manifestation.

2. The Mechanics of Manifestation

Every day we manifest a variety of things—both matter and abstract concepts and situations —by focusing our stream of consciousness. Manifestation is a natural process in which a part of the invisible source energy field is transformed into matter. More accurately, it is when the vibrational frequency of the energy is slowed enough to become visible as matter. The manifestation process is directed through the activities of various layers of consciousness including our personal consciousness, subconsciousness, unconsciousness and the broader collective consciousness. Generally, most people are oblivious to how the majority of manifestations happen because they are directed from parts of their consciousness they are unaware of. When manifestations are caused by their subconsciousness, unconsciousness or the broader collective consciousness, they don't always make the causal connection from the thoughts and/or beliefs to the resulting manifestation. You can and do manifest both deliberately as well as unconsciously. This book focuses more on how to deliberately manifest versus unconscious manifestation. Deliberate manifestation best demonstrates that you have always been in control of your existence and you create your own reality.

The mechanics of manifestation could also be compared with the cause-and-effect principle of **karma**. Karma correlates an individual's intentions and actions with future consequences. Good intentions and good actions create good karma and future happiness, while bad intentions and bad actions create bad karma and future suffering. The Principle of Manifestation connects your thought and beliefs to future manifestations. Positive thoughts create positive manifestations and negative thoughts create negative manifestations.

> Karma, when properly understood,
> is just the mechanics through which consciousness manifests.
> —Deepak Chopra

In a similar way, the proverb "As you sow, so shall you reap" sums up the Principle of Manifestation. What you are sowing is what you chose to think and believe. You then reap the manifestations of your thoughts and beliefs.

> The human race is evolving to the realization
> that what is happening on the level of consciousness
> both precedes and determines what happens in the world.
> —Marianne Williamson

Humans and other sentient beings manifest much of their reality with thoughts and beliefs through their various layers of consciousness. The balance of the universe is manifested through the both lower consciousness and higher collective consciousness. All consciousness is connected and is contained in the collective consciousness.

It is important to understand how the mechanics of manifestation work. Note when something you desire or focus on manifests quickly, then identify what actually happened to facilitate this. Ask yourself how did this manifest so easily? Break down the process of what you thought and how it made you feel, then note what works and what does not. You will always manifest what you think and believe, but that may or may not be what you actually want. If you are unhappy with your manifested reality, identify the sources in your consciousness and make adjustments to those thoughts and/or beliefs.

Components of Deliberate Manifestation

There are three significant components of successful deliberate manifestation. Understanding these components and then managing your consciousness accordingly will lead to mastering the Principle of Manifestation. I will briefly explain the three components in this section and then more thoroughly explain how to implement them in the final chapter, **Living the Principle of Manifestation**.

- A. **Alignment of Consciousness**
- B. **Desire Deliberately**
- C. **Believe and Allow Manifestation**

A. Alignment of Consciousness

To source and bring forth your manifestations, you need to align your personal stream of consciousness with the collective consciousness. This is your access point to source energy field. The source energy field is a higher, infinite field of collective awareness energy. The collective awareness is omnipresent, transcending both space and time; it is all knowing, all powerful and a state of natural bliss. The collective awareness extends beyond the human understanding of awareness. The source energy field contains everyone, everything and every experience that has ever or will ever exist.

Alignment is expanding your lower, limited, personal consciousness to align with and tap into your higher collective consciousness. Alignment is also being in "the zone" or in "the flow" and is a state of instinctive knowing without thinking. This is also recognized as being one with the Universe/God and embracing all of the powers that come from this Oneness. You are always connected to the source energy field/collective consciousness, but depending upon your thoughts and beliefs, you may or may not allow the energy to flow through you to manifest with ease. It is important to recognize that conflicts and distractions in your personal consciousness (misalignment) affect all manifestations, whether they are individual or collective.

Every possible physical manifestation first exists as invisible, faster vibrating energy in the source energy field. Everything is possible in the infinite energy field. If your personal consciousness is aligned with the source energy field, your desired manifestations will be brought into physical reality with relative ease. If you are misaligned with the source energy field, you will struggle to manifest your desires and will often manifest unwanted things instead.

The source energy field has been identified in numerous ways through science, religion and metaphysics. This invisible, omnipresent, energy field is infinite and eternal, and transcends both space and time. It is important to note that the source energy field is an extremely complex concept to comprehend. As a result, man has formulated a wide range of terms to identify it. Some of the terms used don't actually explain the source energy field, but rather identify your point of access to the field. How you chose to identify the energy field will determine the best way for you to understand and achieve alignment. Here are some of the more common terms that identify the source energy field or its point of access. These names all recognize the same infinite energy field that contains everyone and everything— physical and nonphysical or "**all that is.**"

Various Terms for the Source Energy Field

- Quantum Energy Field
- The Universe
- Collective Consciousness or Collective Awareness
- Universal Consciousness or Universal Mind
- Higher Consciousness
- Super Consciousness
- Christ Consciousness
- Divine Consciousness
- God or any variation of the Divine

> I know that you are part of me and I am part of you
> because we are all aspects of the same infinite consciousness
> that we call God and Creation.
> —David Icke

> Everything comes from everything,
> and everything is made out of everything,
> and everything returns into everything.
> —Leonardo da Vinci

Alignment is expanding awareness from your limited personal consciousness (ego awareness) to tap into the higher collective consciousness (infinite awareness). This expansion of awareness has been identified and practiced by many methods depending on the understanding of the source energy field. Here are several of the more notable ways to align with your higher consciousness.

Consciousness Alignment Methods and Practices

- Meditation or Contemplation in various forms
- Yoga: aligning the body, mind and spirit
- Mysticism: union with God or the Divine
- Spirituality, both religious and non-religious
- Seeking Enlightenment

- Experiencing Oneness with the Universe
- Positive Thinking
- Mindfulness or Present Moment Awareness
- Introspection or Self-Examination
- Being in the Zone or the Flow

Some of the most notable masters of manifestation are individuals who achieve and maintained their alignment with the source energy field/collective consciousness. These people are credited with manifesting miracles and other super-human accomplishments, and were often recognized as enlightened beings. Krishna, Buddha, Moses, Elijah and many others credited with performing miracles did so by consistently maintaining their consciousness alignment. Alignment with the source energy field is our natural state of higher consciousness and is accessible for anyone willing to expand their mind and raise their awareness.

> The key to growth is the introduction
> of higher dimensions of consciousness into our awareness.
> —Lao Tzu

> Meditation is to dive all the way within, beyond thought,
> to the source of thought and pure consciousness.
> It enlarges the container, every time you transcend.
> When you come out, you come out refreshed,
> filled with energy and enthusiasm for life.
> —David Lynch

There are techniques of Buddhism, such as meditation,
that anyone can adopt. And, of course,
there are Christian monks and nuns who already use
Buddhist methods in order to develop
their devotion, compassion, and ability to forgive.
—Dalai Lama XIV

Meditation is a vital practice to access conscious contact
with your highest self.
—Wayne Dyer

Mind is consciousness which has put on limitations.
You are originally unlimited and perfect.
Later you take on limitations and become the mind.
—Ramana Maharshi

How do you know if your personal consciousness is aligned to the collective consciousness/source energy field? You can determine your alignment by being mindful of your emotional state. Your emotions signal how you are thinking and whether your consciousness is aligned. You are aligned when you emotionally feel anything positive. Feelings such as peace, calm, gratitude or love all indicate harmony and alignment with the collective consciousness. On the contrary, anything that feels negative signals misalignment. Feelings such as boredom, irritation, regret or hatred all indicate conflict and misalignment with the collective consciousness. Misalignment means you are restricting your connection to the power of the source energy field, and this will adversely affect your ability to deliberately manifest.

> Gratitude is an attitude
> that hooks us up to our source of supply.
> And the more grateful you are,
> the closer you become to your maker,
> to the architect of the universe,
> to the spiritual core of your being.
> It's a phenomenal lesson.
> —Bob Proctor

> It's really important that you feel good.
> Because this feeling good is what goes out as a signal
> into the universe and starts to attract more of itself to you.
> So the more you can feel good,
> the more you will attract the things that help you feel good
> and that will keep bringing you up higher and higher.
> —Joe Vitale

> Our natural state of being is joy.
> It takes so much energy to think negative thoughts
> to speak negative words, to feel miserable.
> The easy path is good thoughts, good words, and good deeds.
> Take the easy path.
> —Rhonda Byrne

> The main event has never been the manifestation;
> the main event has always been the way you feel moment by moment,
> because that's what life is.
> —Esther Hicks

Consciousness alignment is a state of happiness, joy, peace, knowing, contentment, pleasure and nirvana. It is its own reward. Ultimately you can make your goal to direct your consciousness and feel emotionally positive to the best of your abilities. It doesn't matter how you get to this positive, expanded awareness. Whether you choose to do so through mediation, religious devotions, Oneness, understanding of quantum mechanics or any other way, just strive to feel emotionally positive. This is the natural state of our higher collective consciousness, and it opens your connection to the infinite knowing and the infinite power of the source energy field.

B. Desire Deliberately

Once you are aligned properly and feeling the positive emotional confirmation, it is the optimal time to proactively focus on a desire you wish to experience. Manifestation is driven by desire in all of its many forms. Nearly any thought or even point of mental focus can be translated to a desire. That desire then signals the collective consciousness to manifest it. However, not every desire fully manifests for a variety of reasons. If your desire is weak, unfocused or not held long enough, it may stall before it manifests. If you desire anything and it feels negative, it could be an indication that on a conscious or unconscious level that you have a conflicting thought/belief canceling out the manifestation. The negative emotional feeling signals the desired manifestation is not coming because you may be manifesting a block to your original desire. We can also sometimes fixate on something unpleasant and then cause it to unconsciously manifest. You manifest both negatively and positively but if you wish to enjoy a positive experience, understand that it begins with positive desire.

You can actively select a deliberate desire or you can passively desire by focusing on something you are exposed to. If held long enough, a mental fixation—whether active or passive can launch a manifestation. Passively focusing is more often unconscious and could lead to manifesting something unwanted by default. Your mental focus may fixate on something you are annoyed with but don't actually want. This is the downside of an undisciplined mind that aimlessly wanders. All possibilities exist in the collective consciousness/source energy field and are available to manifest. Once you focus on any of these possibilities it begins to slow the nonphysical energy that will materialize, when its vibrational frequency sufficiently decelerates. The longer and clearer the desire/focus, the faster it manifests.

> When you send out a powerful thought into the universe, you send out ripples to all parts of it which come back to you, reflecting what it is you sent out.
> —Stephen Richards

> You can develop a burning desire to succeed. How? Keep your mind on the things you want and off the things you don't want.
> —W. Clement Stone

It is the visionaries, dreamers and planners who will most likely succeed in mastering the Principle of Manifestation because they most often deliberately choose their desires. They are willing to fearlessly dream, plan, set goals and strive for more, all while actively choosing desires with the belief that anything is possible. Life without desire is joyless. Life without fulfilled desire is painful. Mastering manifestation of our desires is one of the most satisfying experiences in physical reality.

> The key to success is to focus our conscious mind
> on things we desire not things we fear.
> —Brian Tracy

> Is your fear of failure greater
> than your desire to succeed?
> —Zig Ziglar

C. Believe and Allow Manifestation

The third component of manifestation is to believe and allow your desire to materialize. Have faith that your higher collective consciousness/source energy field will deliver the appropriate manifestation, when your personal consciousness clearly decides what you want. Believing will prevent possible conflicting manifestations or other blocks. Believing and allowing is a variation of consciousness alignment and will result in a positive emotional feeling. Be mindful of any negative emotions that could signal doubt, anxiety or fear. When you believe and allow, you are called upon to have faith and trust in yourself and your higher collective consciousness. Recognize and believe that you can manifest anything you desire.

Magic is believing in yourself,
if you can do that, you can make anything happen.
—Johann Wolfgang von Goethe

We all have our own life to pursue,
our own kind of dream to be weaving,
and we all have the power to make wishes come true,
as long as we keep believing.
—Louisa May Alcott

Every person is the creation of himself,
the image of his own thinking and believing.
As individuals think and believe, so they are.
—Claude M. Bristol

Dreams are like the paints of a great artist.
Your dreams are your paints, the world is your canvas.
Believing is the brush that converts your dreams
into a masterpiece of reality.
—Anonymous

When you believe in a thing,
believe in it all the way,
implicitly and unquestionable.
—Walt Disney

Believe that life is worth living and your belief
will help create the fact.
—William James

Don't worry about making something happen, just desire it without resistance and allow it to happen. Your resistance (misalignment) to the source energy field can and does stall or stop manifestation. Allowing is letting the power of the source energy field to flow through you to manifest your desires. Allowing and receiving may also require a posture of openness and nonjudgment. There are infinite ways a desire can manifest, and your desire could materialize in an unconventional way.

> It is not your job to make something happen
> —Universal Forces are in place for all of that.
> Your work is to simply determine what you want.
> —Esther Hicks

> You block your dream when you allow your fear
> to grow bigger than your faith.
> —Mary Manin Morrissey

Summary of the Mechanics of Manifestation

The outer physical reality is a direct reflection of your inner consciousness. Changing your outer reality occurs only when you chose to change your inner desires and beliefs through your stream of consciousness. The three components of manifestation—**Alignment, Desire** and **Belief**—involve managing your stream of consciousness to access the power of the collective consciousness. If you master your stream of consciousness, you will master the Principle of Manifestation and be able to create the reality of your dreams.

> One who is connected to the Energy Stream
> is more powerful than a million who are not.
> And two who are harmoniously focused
> and connected to the Energy Stream
> brings about a co-creative endeavor that cannot be matched
> by anything else in all of the Universe.
> —Esther Hicks

> You are a volume in the divine book
> A mirror to the power that created the universe
> Whatever you want, ask it of yourself
> Whatever you're looking for can only be found
> Inside of you.
> —Rumi

> The Universe is the periodical manifestation
> of this unknown Absolute Essence.
> —Helena Blavatsky

3. Living the Principle of Manifestation

Living the Principle of Manifestation is realizing that you control what you manifest in your life and then mastering the process. Mastering manifestation is deliberately creating what you desire versus unconsciously generating things you don't want. To be a successful creator, you need to master the three keys of **Alignment**, **Desire** and **Belief** that facilitate deliberate manifestation.

As humans in this physical reality, we have infinite opportunities to manifest and experience life. We can do this because the physical universe provides an environment where we can transform energy into physical matter. Manifestation may not occur the same way in a nonphysical reality such as the afterlife. We incarnated as humans for the opportunities of the physical experience, and we can make this joyful or painful depending upon our desires and beliefs. The creative process of manifestation gives us godlike powers to create or destroy anything we desire.

> We are not human beings having a spiritual experience.
> We are spiritual beings having a human experience.
> —Pierre Teilhard de Chardin

The three key components of manifestation—**Alignment**, **Desire** and **Belief**—can be experienced numerous ways. Some approaches are inspired by religion, some scientific, some psychological and others philosophical. Any method is acceptable if you achieve your desired manifestation. Your methods should always be guided by your personal preferences. It is also important to note that these three components can be experienced in sequence or simultaneously. Alignment, Desire and Belief all should result with the same positive emotional indicators when practiced correctly. An underlying goal is to always feel positive to confirm your stream of consciousness is aligned with the collective consciousness.

A. Achieving Consciousness Alignment

Consciousness alignment to the source energy field is being in harmony and agreement with it and can be described in several ways depending upon the understanding of the source energy field. Again the source energy field can be identified as our higher collective consciousness; in a religious context this is God or any variation of the

Divine. In scientific terms, the source energy field is explained through quantum mechanics as an infinite quantum energy field that contains everything both physical and nonphysical. Regardless of how you understand the source energy field, your access to it is primarily through the portal of your mind.

Consciousness alignment is encouraging agreement and harmony between your lower personal consciousness (ego awareness) and your higher collective consciousness (infinite awareness). Alignment is expanding your limited personal awareness to access more of the collective awareness energy. Keep in mind that any form of alignment will result in a positive emotional feeling and any form of misalignment will cause a negative emotional feeling. This is consciousness harmony versus consciousness conflict.

Simply put, any thoughts, beliefs or actions that feel positive, confirm alignment while anything that feels negative, confirms misaligned. If you struggle with correcting or changing your negative thoughts and beliefs, simple focus instead on anything that feels emotionally positive. This approach emphasizes *feeling* your way to alignment instead of *thinking* your way to alignment. Your thoughts/beliefs and your emotions are so intertwined that if you change either, you will change both.

To manage consciousness alignment, it is quite beneficial to engage in some form of **mindfulness**. This psychological and spiritual process encourages present moment awareness to your thoughts, emotions and experiences. Mindfulness requires close examination of your current thoughts, beliefs, emotions and experiences to fully understand what your stream of consciousness is manifesting. Recognize your positive or negative emotional signals, and understand what thoughts or beliefs trigger these signals. How well are you in tune with your thoughts and emotions? How sensitive are you to the subtle changes in your thoughts and emotions? Recognize any negative emotions. A cringe, a regret, a discomfort, fear, worry or anxiety—all are a signal that something is off/misaligned in your consciousness. When you identify these negative emotions, immediately make a mental correction. Rationalize and then let go of the negative thoughts or beliefs behind the negative emotions. Or just clear your consciousness of all thoughts (a goal of **mediation**) and redirect your consciousness to a positive thought/belief. This will trigger a positive emotion.

Understand that your natural state of consciousness is complete happiness and bliss. If you believe or feel anything less than that, you are out of sync with your natural state and misaligned with the source energy field.

Your goal should be to drive to the positive emotions of alignment and let go of anything negative and misaligned. Mindfulness ultimately helps you to evaluate and manage your stream of consciousness and adjust toward alignment.

Consciousness alignment or misalignment is neither virtuous nor immoral. Good people often get misaligned, and immoral people can be much aligned. The emotional signals of alignment or misalignment, however, are either pleasant or unpleasant feeling. Alignment is a position of strength that facilitates easier manifestation and as a bonus it feels pleasant. Here are some of the mental states that signal alignment or misalignment of your personal consciousness with the collective consciousness.

Positive Signals of Alignment	**Negative Signals of Misalignment**
Love	Hate
Happiness	Sadness/Depression
Gratitude	Ungrateful
Optimism	Pessimism
Calmness	Frenzy/Panic
Laughter	Sorrow
Humor	Anger

Kindness	**Cruelty**
Patience	**Impatience**
Confidence	**Insecurity**
Knowledge	**Ignorance**
Knowing	**Doubt**
Conviction	**Hesitation**
Courage	**Fear**
Open-mindedness	**Closed-mindedness**
Nonjudgmental	**Judgmental**

The outer world is a direct reflection and projection of your inner consciousness, and you can clearly see if you are aligned or misaligned. If the outer world is turbulent, it is because the choices of your inner consciousness are turbulent. This can be changed if you change your thoughts and beliefs. Master the focus of your consciousness and you will master manifestation.

> Beautify your inner dialogue.
> Beautify your inner world with love light and compassion.
> Life will be beautiful.
> —Amit Ray

> If you always attach positive emotions to the things you want, and never attach negative emotions to the things you don't, then that which you desire most will invariably come your way.
> —Matt D. Miller

> Remember that in the end,
> the universe responds to our emotions,
> not to our words.
> —Stephen Richards

> Non-judgment quiets the internal dialogue,
> and this opens once again the doorway to creativity.
> —Deepak Chopra

> Knowing yourself is the beginning of all wisdom.
> —Aristotle

Any way you choose to align yourself is acceptable, and you should base your choice on your preference. The key to alignment is achieving a positive emotional feeling that signals you are in alignment/agreement with the source energy field. Here are several significant ways to align your consciousness with the source energy field.

- **Meditation** refers to a wide variety of practices that trains one's mind attain a higher level of awareness or consciousness. The meditation practitioner internally regulates their mind in a variety of possible ways, including single point concentration, openness awareness and mindfulness awareness. Mediation can be either stationary (such as sitting) or moving (such as yoga or walking), and practiced individually or guided in a group. Meditation is regularly practiced for the benefits of relaxation, increasing internal energy and the health benefits of reducing blood pressure, reducing anxiety and reducing depression. There is such a wide range of meditation practices that anyone can find a method personally beneficial. Nearly every religion has meditative practices, and each method provides a unique personal experience. I will identify some of the more common types and examples of meditation and their objections. There are hundreds of meditative practices, however, and further research and investigation may be required if you choose to pursue a particular one. Here are the three main types of meditation and a few examples of each.

Types and Examples of Meditation

- **Concentrative Meditation (narrow, single-point focus)**
  Transcendental Meditation
  Samadhi Meditation

- **Open Awareness Meditation (open focus)**
  Zen Mediation
  Shikantaza Meditation

- **Mindfulness Meditation (both narrow and open focus)**
  Vipassana Meditation

Depending upon the meditative practice, there are a variety of objectives that all cultivate alignment with your higher collective consciousness.

Objectives of Meditation

- To quiet the mind and focus on a single awareness instead of many thoughts
- To transcend the mind and thought and experience our core essence
- To attain a state that is free of mental disturbance
- To realize an intuitive understanding of spiritual truths
- To cultivate love, compassion or other empathic attitudes
- To achieve self-realization and/or enlightenment
- To directly experience the Oneness of the Universe
- To experience a Higher Self, Supreme Consciousness or God
- To realize that you are God

One significant objective of many forms of meditation is to quiet and clear your mind of the many thoughts that create noise in your consciousness. "Too many thoughts" are multiple and often conflicting requests for manifestation. Too much mental noise generally stalls or cancels manifestations. You can quiet and clear the mind by either narrowing your mental focus to a single point or opening your mind wide and essentially letting go of all thought. Either way, you are aligning your consciousness to better manifest your next clearly focused desire.

> If you are religious, pray.
> If you are philosophical, contemplate.
> If you are spiritual, meditate.
> —John K. Brown

> Meditation is the dissolution of thoughts
> in eternal awareness or pure consciousness
> without objectification,
> knowing without thinking,
> merging finitude in infinity.
> —Voltaire

> To understand the immeasurable,
> the mind must be extraordinarily quiet, still.
> —Jiddu Krishnamurti

> Meditation is a way for nourishing and blossoming
> the divinity within you.
> —Amit Ray

> Meditation is realizing and expanding
> your inner beauty in every direction.
> —Amit Ray

- **Mysticism** is commonly known as becoming one with God, the Absolute or the Infinite. This union with the Divine may also refer to any kind of altered state of consciousness or ecstasy that involves religious or spiritual significance. Additionally, mysticism can lead to the attainment of ultimate hidden truths and spiritual enlightenment. The mystic path to alignment is usually practiced through love and devotion to God. While mysticism is quite different from the practice of meditation, the destination is the same; both lead to alignment with the higher collective consciousness/God and Oneness with the Universe. When you achieve alignment through mysticism, you realize that you are part of God and can use the power of the Divine to manifest.

> This overcoming of all the usual barriers
> between the individual and the Absolute
> is the great mystic achievement.
> In mystic states we both become one with the Absolute
> and we become aware of our oneness.
> This is the everlasting and triumphant mystical tradition,
> hardly altered by differences of clime or creed.
> —William James

> The eye through which I see God
> is the same eye through which God sees me;
> my eye and God's eye are one eye,
> one seeing, one knowing, one love.
> —Meister Eckhart

> God is all there is—God includes everything,
> all possibility and all action,
> for Spirit is the invisible essence and substance of all form.
> —Ernest Holmes

> To whatever extent your mind is aligned with love,
> you will receive divine compensation
> for any lack in your material existence.
> From spiritual substance will come material manifestation.
> This is not just a theory; it is a fact.
> It is a law by which the universe operates.
> I call it the Law of Divine Compensation.
> —Marianne Williamson

- **Positive Thinking** is a nonreligious, philosophical and psychological approach to alignment with the source energy field. In this mental practice, one rationalizes and encourages positive thoughts instead of accepting a negative outlook. You strive to find the bright side or silver lining in all situations. The general approach is to adopt an attitude of optimism and openness and always seek positive solutions. The use of positive affirmations and positive visualizations also help to reinforce an optimistic approach and attitude. When you reinforce a desire with related positive affirmations and positive thoughts, it is easier to believe that your desire will manifest.

Positive thinking is similar to the **Law of Attraction,** which states that "likes attract likes." Positive thoughts produce/attract positive results, and negative thoughts produce/attract negative results. Positive thinking ultimately leads to positive emotional feelings, which signal alignment with the source energy field/higher consciousness.

> The greatest discovery of all time
> is that a person can change his future
> by merely changing his attitude.
> —Oprah Winfrey

> Man often becomes what he believes himself to be.
> If I keep on saying to myself that I cannot do a certain thing,
> it is possible that I may end
> by really becoming incapable of doing it.
> On the contrary, if I have the belief that I can do it,
> I shall surely acquire the capacity to do it
> even if I may not have it at the beginning.
> —Mahatma Gandhi

> The positive thinker sees the invisible,
> feels the intangible,
> and achieves the impossible.
> —Winston Churchill

> Optimism is the most important human trait,
> because it allows us to evolve our ideas,
> to improve our situation,
> and to hope for a better tomorrow.
> —Seth Godin

> I am more and more convinced that our happiness or unhappiness
> depends far more on the way we meet the events of life
> than on the nature of those events themselves.
> —Karl Wilhelm von Humboldt

- **The Principle of Oneness** explains that everything physical and nonphysical is a single connected infinite, energy field. This intellectual approach to alignment can be explained through science and experienced through spirituality. Comprehending and experiencing the Principle of Oneness is also a path that leads to enlightenment.

The scientific explanation of Oneness is based upon string theory from quantum physics. Everything is a form of energy and on a subatomic level this energy is identical. This identical energy exists in an infinite quantum energy field, but only appears different because of different vibrational frequencies. A good way to visualize this is to think of various forms of water. Ice, snow, fog, rain and invisible moisture are all forms of the water, but manifest differently because of different environmental conditions. Regardless of how it manifests, the core material is all one substance: water. Intellectually believing in the Oneness aligns your personal consciousness with the knowledge of collective consciousness.

The spiritual explanation for Oneness is similar to **mysticism**, or becoming one with God/the Universe. The Principle of Oneness explains that you are literally everyone, everything, in every place and at every time. This is the same concept of God or the Divine being identified as "all that is". Rumi profoundly explained the Principle of Oneness in a succinct poetic thought.

> "You are not a drop in the ocean.
> You are the entire ocean in a drop."

It is important that you emotionally experience the connections of Oneness that signal alignment. This can be achieved through nonjudgment and love of everyone and everything that makes up your broader self. Nonjudgment and love both feel emotionally positive signaling alignment with your higher consciousness. You can feel your connection to everything; the stronger the positive emotional feelings, the greater the alignment to the collective consciousness. It is the power of Oneness that facilitates effortless manifestation.

A person experiences life as
something separated from the rest—
a kind of optical delusion of consciousness.
Our task must be to free ourselves
from this self-imposed prison,
and through compassion,
to find the reality of Oneness.
—Albert Einstein

Quantum physics thus reveals
a basic oneness of the universe.
—Erwin Schrödinger

We are here to awaken
from the illusion of our separateness.
—Thich Nhat Hanh

All differences in this world
are of degree, and not of kind,
because oneness is the secret of everything.
—Swami Vivekananda

We are all connected
to everyone and everything in the universe.
Therefore, everything one does as an individual
affects the whole.
All thoughts, words, images, prayers, blessings,
and deeds are listened to by all that is.
—Serge Kahili King

Simply see that you are at the center of the universe,
and accept all things and beings
as parts of your infinite body.
When you perceive that an act done to another
is done to yourself,
you have understood the great truth.
—Lao Tzu

Those who are highly evolved,
maintain an undiscriminating perception.
Seeing everything, labeling nothing,
they maintain their awareness of the Great Oneness.
Thus they are supported by it.
—Lao Tzu

You are the Universe expressing itself
as a human for a little while.
—Eckhart Tolle

Stop acting so small.
You are the Universe in ecstatic motion.
—Rumi

Do not feel lonely,
the entire Universe is inside you.
—Rumi

Summary of Achieving Consciousness Alignment

The purpose of alignment is to expand the connection of your personal consciousness to the source energy field/your higher collective consciousness. This alignment of consciousness then helps to facilitate manifestation with ease. Alignment to the source energy field can be achieved by many practices including meditation, mysticism, positive thoughts and experiencing the Principle of Oneness. Regardless of the practice, alignment will feel emotionally positive. The second you are feeling anything negative, adjust your thoughts and beliefs to change your emotions.

The thoughts of your consciousness are so intertwined with your emotions that if you change either, you change both. If you can't identify and transcend the negative thought producing the negative emotion, just detach from or shift from the negative emotion. Feel/emote and believe your way back to a positive emotional state and your stream of consciousness will follow. This is an internal mental and emotional process and may require ignoring the negativity of the physical world, as you shift to alignment.

The positive emotions of alignment do not depend on our circumstances, but rather are a result of the way we intellectually and emotionally interpret our life situations. Ultimately, our chosen attitude will override any circumstance, whether positive or negative. Once again, our emotions are resulting indicators of personal consciousness choosing to focus on thoughts and beliefs that are either aligned (positive) or misaligned (negative). Your goal should be to get aligned and stay aligned. When you are, you will be in your most powerful position to facilitate manifestation.

B. Desire Deliberately

Desire is the second key component to the manifestation process. Desire is having a strong feeling of wanting something, someone or a particular outcome. Desire is a longing to have or experience another aspect of your broader self. When you contemplate the seemingly separate aspects of the Universe, you desire to connect with some of those aspects. Desire is an act of inclusion, love and ultimately, the recognition of Oneness. If you fully understand and experience Oneness (achieve enlightenment), your propensity for desire will diminish because you will already experience your connection to everything.

Desires can be active or passive choices from our personal consciousness and can develop from a variety of mental activities. Any thought, visualization, fixation or focus of attention can form a desire and could possibly launch a manifestation. Some desires are deliberate selections; others are unconscious mental fixation. Whether we realize it or not, we are constantly choosing desires and launching manifestations.

We are here to explore our desires, and it is through them that we have manifested ourselves and incarnated in human form. The human experience and physical reality then provides further opportunity to manifest and experience our desires. Manifestation can be a creative and joyful process. There is often a euphoric feeling when desiring and a satisfaction when it manifests.

> When a person really desires something,
> all the universe conspires
> to help that person to realize his dream.
> —Paulo Coelho

> We are desire.
> It is the essence of the human Soul,
> the secret of our existence.
> Absolutely nothing of human greatness
> is ever accomplished without it.
> Not a symphony has been written, a mountain climbed,

an injustice fought, or a love sustained apart from desire.
Desire fuels our search for the life we prize.
—John Elderidge

Desire is a teacher:
When we immerse ourselves in it without guilt,
shame, or clinging,
it can show us something special about our own minds
that allows us to embrace life fully.
—Mark Epstein

When your desires are strong enough
you will appear to possess superhuman powers to achieve.
—Napoleon Hill

Desire is the starting point of all achievement,
not a hope, not a wish,
but a keen pulsating desire which transcends everything.
—Napoleon Hill

Plant the seed of desire in your mind
and it forms a nucleus with power to attract to itself
everything needed for its fulfillment.
—Robert Collier

Managing Deliberate Desires to Manifest

How you desire effects whether it will manifest. We are constantly launching manifestations with our mental activities from various levels of consciousness. We can manifest deliberately or unconsciously; both approaches have benefits and shortcomings. If you are open and enjoy an element of surprise, you may choose to manifest more unconsciously by default. If you appreciate more control, however, you may prefer to manifest consciously and deliberately. Deliberate manifestations require managing your stream of consciousness and deliberately selecting your desires.

These are the keys to managing deliberate desires to manifest.

1. **Desire deliberately verse unconsciously.**

   Deliberate desire is an active mental decision verse a passive unconscious mental focus. It is surprising how few people actually know and choose what they desire and thus struggle to manifest deliberately. Pay close attention to your mind mental focus. Focus on what you desire and ignore the things you dislike. Internally make a mental choice of what you desire versus mirroring things you observe in your environment. Deliberate desire encourages proactive, thoughtful manifestation versus unconscious and unwanted manifestation.

Be *for* something instead of pushing *against* something. Any focus on something you don't want signals to the Universe to bring forth the object of your fixation. The source energy field/collective consciousness doesn't recognize your aversion to something; it just recognizes what your consciousness focuses on. Purposely choose your desires instead of letting your mind wander and launch unwanted manifestations.

> Where Attention goes Energy flows;
> Where Intention goes Energy flows!
> —James Redfield

> The universe does not know
> whether the vibration that you're offering
> is because of something you're observing
> or something you're remembering
> or something that you are imagining.
> It just receives the vibration and answers it
> with things that match it.
> —Esther Hicks

2. **Avoid launching conflicting manifestations.**

If you want something, but at the same time think or believe you cannot achieve it, your doubts and conflicting beliefs will cancel out your desire. You are essentially launching two different conflicting manifestations that cancel each other out. Be mentally aware of when you are launching conflicting manifestations.

You will feel when doubts and conflicting thoughts are in play because the normal positive emotions of a desire will turn negative and unpleasant. You will sense that your desire is not going to happen and you will feel unhappy. It is very common to want something such as a new job and at the same time not be open for change. Your aversion to change is actually a desire for nothing to happen, and this could cancel out the desire for a new job. The end result is that nothing manifests. When you are struggling to manifest something, pause and ask yourself why am I not allowing this to happen? What else am I manifesting that is canceling my original desire? Your remedy is to identify and eliminate the doubts or conflicting beliefs, effectively voiding the contradictory manifestations. Then your original desire will be free to manifest.

> Doubt kills more dreams than failure ever will.
> —Suzy Kassem

> As long as you are feeling discomfort within anything,
> you're holding yourself in a vibration
> where all of the things that you have conjured,

and all of the things that you have
let the Universe know that you want,
cannot flow to you.
—Esther Hicks

Every mental act is composed of doubt and belief,
but it is belief that is the positive,
it is belief that sustains thought and holds the world together.
—Søren Kierkegaard

The only limit to our realization of tomorrow
will be our doubts of today.
Let us move forward with strong and active faith.
—Franklin D. Roosevelt

Manifesting your desires requires an understanding
of the universe's abundance and inherently giving nature.
If you ask from a position of fear or desperation,
you are sending out your fear and desperation,
and the universe, giving, reflecting,
and non-judgmental as it is,
will send those right back at you.
—Stephen Richards

3. **Focus on having instead of wanting.**

You will not manifest the object of desire if you focus on the state of wanting or lacking. If you focus on state of lacking, your consciousness will manifest the continuation of this state. Deliberately desire something, then immediately focus on how positive it feels to have it. Visualize having your desire versus wanting your desire. See it in your mind and emotionally feel the positive energy of having your desire. You will not manifest a solution focusing on the problem. Have the mental discipline to keep your eye (mental focus) on the prize (the outcome) and you will manifest your desire with relative ease.

> As soon as you stop wanting something,
> you get it.
> —Andy Warhol

> We can not solve our problems
> with the same level of thinking that created them.
> —Albert Einstein

> To conquer frustration,
> one must remain intensely focused on the outcome,
> not the obstacles.
> —T. F. Hodge

> You get there by realizing you are already there.
> —Eckhart Tolle

> To bring anything into your life,
> imagine that it's already there.
> —Richard Bach

> I am the greatest,
> I said that even before I knew I was.
> —Muhammad Ali

4. **Maintain consistent mental focus on the desire until it manifests.**

Many people lack consistent focused desires, and they want various things for short periods of time. They often abandon any unfulfilled desires for a new desire. This can be caused by impatience, lack of focus or fear of failure. Don't panic, however, and don't compromise with an alternate desire while waiting for your initial one. This will split your consciousness energy and will result in few if any deliberate manifestations. Maintain a consistent mental focus on your desire until it materializes, while ignoring anything that distracts from what you want. The most successful creators are single focused. Maintain your mental focus until your desire is fully manifested.

> The successful warrior is the average man,
> with laser-like focus.
> —Bruce Lee

> One essential to success is that your desire
> be an all-obsessing one,

your thoughts and aim be coordinated,
and your energy be concentrated and applied without letup.
—Claude M. Bristol

Focus on your goals, not your fear.
Focus like a laser beam on your goals.
—Roy T. Bennett

If you chase two rabbits, both will escape.
—Anonymous

The shorter way to do many things
is to do only one thing at a time.
—Wolfgang Amadeus Mozart

Most people have no idea of the giant capacity
we can immediately command when we focus
all of our resources on mastering a single area of our lives.
—Anthony Robbins

Someone who cannot reign in his thoughts and focus
can never achieve anything he wants.
On the other hand, a man who has the ability
to align his thoughts and devote complete focus
and concentration on the task at hand
can realize anything that he aspires to.
—David Hewitt

As a single footstep will not make a path on the earth,
so a single thought will not make a pathway in the mind.
To make a deep physical path, we walk again and again.

> To make a deep mental path, we must think over and over
> the kind of thoughts we wish to dominate our lives.
> —Henry David Thoreau

5. **At least two forms of energy are required to manifest matter.**

    According to quantum mechanics, at least two forms of energy are required to create physical matter. A single form of energy must have something to collide with to slow its vibrational frequency and manifest as matter. This is the same principle applies to manifestation with the energies of thoughts, beliefs and desires. This law of two or more forms of energy (thoughts/beliefs) is a safety mechanism of our higher collective consciousness to prevent random, singular thoughts from manifesting. We process as many as 50,000 thoughts each day. If all those manifested immediately, the results would be chaotic.

    In quantum mechanics, two or more positively charged energy particles can collide, manifesting positively charged matter. Two or more negatively charged energy particles (antiparticles) can join, manifesting negatively charged matter (antimatter). When positive and negative energy particles come together, they annihilate each other. The energy of the particles is released back into the source energy field, but nothing manifests.

In the Principle of Manifestation, two or more positive thoughts/desires (energies) can create a positive physical manifestation and two or more negative thoughts/desires (energies) can create a negative physical manifestation. The combination of a positive and a negative energy will cancel (annihilate) manifestation. Alignment already provides one point of positive energy to collide with a positive desire to produce the positive physical manifestation.

A positive manifestation from consciousness is something you will emotionally enjoy and a negative manifestation you will not enjoy. The emotional feelings you have as you focus on a desire, signal if the potential manifestation will be positive or negative. The Universe will not stop a negative manifestation but the unpleasant, negative feelings at the point of desire, are your warning signs of what is coming.

Constantly monitor your thoughts and emotions so you are aware of what you are manifesting. If your reality is not what you intended to create, change your thoughts. If your reality feels unpleasant, redirect your stream of consciousness to positive thoughts. Also, plant multiple positive thoughts in your stream of consciousness to prevent any negative thoughts from occupying your mind. This is proactive positive thinking versus reactive negative thinking. There is significant power in positive thinking and optimism versus negative thinking and pessimism.

> Energy is liberated matter,
> matter is energy waiting to happen.
> —Bill Bryson

> Once you replace negative thoughts with positive ones,
> you'll start having positive results.
> —Willie Nelson

> Be vigilant;
> guard your mind against negative thoughts.
> —Buddha

> Learning to distance yourself from all the negativity
> is one of the greatest lessons to achieve inner peace.
> —Roy T. Bennett

> To give your positive or negative attention to something
> is a way of giving energy.
> The most damaging form of behavior
> is withholding your attention.
> —Masaru Emoto

> There is little difference in people,
> but that little difference makes a big difference.
> The little difference is attitude.
> The big difference is whether it is positive or negative.
> —W. Clement Stone

Are there any limitations to what can be manifested?

The short answer to the question is yes and no. Anything and everything can be manifested. The catch, however, is that we can and do collectively manifest limitations to our own abilities. These limitations can be both beneficial and detrimental to our happiness. Some of the beneficial limitations we manifest include the laws of physics. The manifested limitations of both space and time provide a sense of order and predictability in our physical environment. Our physical incarnation and lifespan is also a limitation of our infinite collective consciousness. Other parts of our collective consciousness choose the limitations of animals, plants or various inanimate objects to experience the physical reality. If we did not limit our infinite collective consciousness, we would not experience the individuality of the physical world and only experience the energetic existence in the nonphysical source energy field. In the source energy field all our personal consciousnesses coalesce and are indistinguishable.

The laws of physics in any reality are not static or absolute. As a result these limitations can be altered by both our personal or collective consciousness. In human history, there are many examples of individuals—especially enlightened ones—who have altered the laws of physics and performed what appear to be miracles. This is possible for anyone who can manage their stream of consciousness with deliberate desire and belief.

> We have no right to assume that any physical laws exist,
> or if they have existed up until now,
> that they will continue to exist
> in a similar manner in the future.
> —Max Planck

Some limitations are beneficial, while others prevent us from manifesting our true desires. Ironically, we have the power to make ourselves powerless when we manifest certain limitations. If you believe you are weak and powerless, you will manifest that reality. Limitations of power, self-esteem, value and ability, serve only to limit our manifestation skills and prevent us from fulfilling our desires.

These limitations are often the result of negativity and fear-based beliefs. The fear of success, fear of failure and even the fear of too many possibilities can be the root cause of certain limitations. These types of self-inflicted limitations can result in feelings of despair and unhappiness. Often times, we are unaware of all the limitations we manifest. Be mindful of what limitations you manifest with your thoughts and beliefs. You may be surprised how often you verbally articulate limitations. Whenever you say: I can't do this—that will never work—I don't understand this—I'm not good at that......, you have articulated a belief that manifests a limitation. Any limitation can be removed by changing your attitude. Change your thoughts and beliefs and the limitation will be gone.

Believe in your infinite potential.
Your only limitations are those you set upon yourself.
—Roy T. Bennett

You will become as small as your controlling desire;
as great as your dominant aspiration.
—James Allen

Mind is consciousness which has put on limitations.
You are originally unlimited and perfect.
Later you take on limitations and become the mind.
—Ramana Maharshi

> Life has no limitations, except the ones you make.
> —Les Brown

> Argue for your limitations, and sure enough they're yours.
> —Richard Bach

> The greatest progress in life
> is when you know your limitations,
> and then you have the courage to drop them.
> —Yogi Bhajan

Summary of Desire

Desire is an expression of longing to connect with other aspects of our broader self. It is through desire that we manifest various parts of source energy field to know and experience these parts of ourselves. Enjoy your desires and the creative process of manifestation. Desire deliberately and positively, maintaining your focus without manifesting a conflict or limitation, until your original desire manifests.

We have manifested ourselves through the collective consciousness/source energy field and we have chosen the physical form to allow us to more opportunities to manifest. Whether you are an artist, musician, inventor, builder, farmer, philosopher, writer, parent or anything else, you are a creator of the physical reality. Desire is merely our way of identifying what we want to manifest.

Here are the key points to understanding and managing desires to manifest.

- **Desire is longing to experience Oneness.**
- **Desire deliberately verse unconsciously.**
- **Avoid launching conflicting manifestations.**
- **Focus on having instead of wanting.**
- **Maintain consistent mental focus on the desire until it manifests.**
- **At least two forms of energy are required to manifest matter.**
- **The only limitations to manifestations are the ones we manifest.**

C. Believe and Allow Manifestation

The final component of manifestation is to believe and allow your desires to materialize. This is when you trust that what you desire can and will manifest. This trust is rooted in core beliefs both conscious and subconscious. Believing is also another form of consciousness alignment and will feel emotionally positive. Belief leads to an intuitive knowledge that your desires will manifest. You will sense that what you want is coming your way.

Believing your desire will manifest is predicated upon your system of core beliefs. Beliefs are thoughts that you trust are true and core beliefs are any beliefs that are central to your world view. Your core beliefs are fundamental to the formation of your sphere of reality. Truth and logic are not necessary to form a core belief. Core beliefs can be established on either a conscious or subconscious level and are personal choices of how you view, evaluate and create your reality. Ultimately it is what you believe that allows your desires manifest.

> You manifest what you believe,
> not what you want.
> —Sonia Ricotti

Why believe consciousness controls manifestation?

There are many reasons to believe you can manifest anything you desire. This is not a new concept, and there is a rich scientific, philosophic and spiritual history of the connection of consciousness and matter. Here are three significant examples supporting the Principle of Manifestation.

- Personal observations are possible the most compelling support for why we should believe we control manifestation. We manifest every day. If you are mindful, you can easily see the cause and effect of your stream of consciousness to the reality you experience. The more mindful you are, the more you will see the connections of mind and matter. As you learn to control and direct your stream of consciousness, you will see the results in your reality. There are no coincidences in life, and everything happens for a reason. The reason is your choices of beliefs and desires in your stream of consciousness.

> Coincidence is the word we use
> when we can't see the levers and pulleys.
> —Emma Bull

> You cannot have a positive life
> and a negative mind.
> —Joyce Meyer

> We are shaped by our thoughts;
> we become what we think.
> When the mind is pure,
> joy follows like a shadow that never leaves.
> —Buddha

- Quantum physics explains that when two or more forms of energy collide, physical matter can manifest. This was originally only a theory, but later scientists successfully collided photons (massless light energy) and produced matter particles (positively charged electrons). Thoughts, desires and beliefs are all forms of massless energy that originate from your consciousness. Your desire for something can collide with your belief that you will have it and thus manifest the object of desire. Quantum physics supports the concept of material manifestation through colliding energies and this supports the Principle of Manifestation.

A fundamental conclusion of the new physics
also acknowledges that the observer creates the reality.
As observers, we are personally involved
with the creation of our own reality.
Physicists are being forced to admit
that the universe is a "mental" construction.
Pioneering physicist Sir James Jeans wrote:
"The stream of knowledge is heading toward
a non-mechanical reality; the universe begins to look
more like a great thought than like a great machine.
Mind no longer appears to be an accidental intruder
into the realm of matter, we ought rather hail it
as the creator and governor of the realm of matter.
Get over it, and accept the inarguable conclusion.
The universe is immaterial-mental and spiritual.
—Richard Conn Henry

- According to various religions, God is the source of all manifestation. The collective consciousness/source energy field is also known as God, and we are both part and all of this. As part of God, we have the power of the Divine and thus can manifest anything we can desire. Regardless of whether you believe you are God or that God works through you, the power to manifest has always been there. Recognize and believe that you are completely in control of your manifestations.

> He said to them, "Because of your little faith.
> For truly I tell you,
> if you have faith the size of a mustard seed,
> you will say to this mountain,
> 'Move from here to there,' and it will move;
> and nothing will be impossible for you."
> —Jesus, Matthew 17:20 (NRSV)

Allowing Manifestation

Allowing is letting the power of the source energy field flow without resistance and is a reflection of trust in the collective consciousness. As a manifestation begins to materialize, you have the choice to trust and allow it, or cancel it. Recognize that your manifestation could arrive in a creative and unexpected form. Be open and allow your desire come into existence, then accept what you manifest without anxiety or guilt. Be careful not to cancel a desired manifestation with judgments of unworthiness. Because of the Oneness of everything, you are taking from yourself and giving back to yourself. You deserve whatever you desire.

Allowing generally involves two other principles of enlightenment, Openness and Nonjudgment. On a much higher level, try to allow everything in the physical universe to exist as it is, without judgment. Judgment, anger, disapproval and even annoyance are all indications that you are misaligning and restricting your connection to the source energy field. This misalignment will adversely affect your ability to consciously manifest. Remember that misaligned can cancel manifestation or launch a negative manifestation.

Summary of Believing and Allowing Manifestation

Believing and allowing is trusting that you can manifest your desires and accepting them when they materialize. This component of manifestation is also your opportunity to reaffirm your alignment with the collective consciousness as the source of manifestation.

The connection of consciousness to manifestation has been explained throughout history using science, philosophy and religion. Believing in the ability to manifest can then be rationalized in at least three different ways.

- Personal Observations of Reality
- Quantum Physics
- Religious References

Regardless of how or why you believe, it is a critical component to the manifestation process. A belief is a habitual thought that you trust is true. Ultimately, you manifest only what you believe whether that belief is conscious or subconscious. Your beliefs have a greater influence on the manifestation because they are more habitual and ingrained in your consciousness than a random thought that comes in and out of your mind. Perhaps the most important thing you can do to master manifestation is to be aware of what you choose to believe and how those beliefs influence what you want to manifest in your life.

> Repetition of the same chant, the same incantations,
> the same affirmations leads to belief,
> and once that belief becomes a deep conviction,
> things begin to happen.
> —Claude M. Bristol

> You must start with desire,
> keeping in mind that with the magic of believing
> you can obtain what you picture in your mind's eye.
> —Claude M. Bristol

Summary of Living the Principle of Manifestation

Living and mastering the Principle of Manifestations starts with allowing yourself the joy of desiring anything you want. Manifestation is the empowering process of transforming energy to matter by directing your consciousness with your mind. Focus your thoughts, beliefs and desires on the things you really want, then believe in your ability to materialize them.

The Principle of Manifestation involves managing your stream of consciousness to direct the conversion of energy into matter. The three components of Alignment, Desire and Belief all involve managing your stream of consciousness.

1. **Align your personal consciousness with the collective consciousness/source energy field/God.** This is the essence of who you are and the basis for your power to create and manifest.

2. **Desire deliberately, without conflict and stay focused on your desire until it manifests.** This is where you direct the source energy to manifest what you want.

3. **Believe that you can manifest anything you desire, then allow it to materialize.** You are part of and all of the collective consciousness/source energy field/God and have the power to manifest anything you desire.

As you begin to master the Principle of Manifestation you will realize that you create and control everything in your life. This power has always been yours whether you realize it or not. You create and control reality with your consciousness and access it through your mind. When your consciousness is aligned to the infinite knowledge and power of the collective consciousness/source energy field/God and you allow it to flow through you, you can manifest anything you desire. When you control and direct your stream of consciousness, you will master the Principle of Manifestation.

The universe is but a partial manifestation
of your limitless capacity to become.
—Sri Nisargadatta Maharaj

You are what you want to become.
Why search anymore?
You are a wonderful manifestation.
The whole universe has come together
to make your existence possible.
There is nothing that is not you.
The kingdom of God, the Pure Land,
nirvana, happiness, and liberation
are all you.
—Thich Nhat Hanh

We are what we think.
All that we are arises with our thoughts.
With our thoughts,
we make the world.
—Buddha

Special Message to the Reader

IF YOU APPRECIATE THE TRUTH and wisdom of this book, keep it as a reference guide on your path to enlightenment. Use *The Principle of Manifestation* as a key to interpret other works of wisdom, helping to unlock their deeper meanings. Live and experience your ability to deliberately manifest and feel the joy and bliss that results. Help spread the word by sharing this knowledge. Speak with others, or submit a book review that notes how this principle can enrich your life. Gift a copy of this book to anyone you believe could benefit from its knowledge and wisdom. One of the greatest things we can do is to inspire others.

Thank you for helping enlighten the world.

Russell Anthony Gibbs

RussellAnthonyGibbs.com

About the Author

AWARD-WINNING AND BESTSELLING AUTHOR RUSSELL Anthony Gibbs is a philosopher and spiritual seeker on a quest for enlightenment. His critically acclaimed first book, *The Six Principles of Enlightenment and Meaning of Life*, won the **2016 Pinnacle Book Achievement Award for Best Book in Spiritual Self Help.** *The Six Principles* is a comprehensive overview of the fundamentals of enlightenment and is the first of an eight-book series. This book, ***The Principle of Manifestation***, is the third in the series.

Gibbs grew up in a huge family—one of eleven children—on a farm in Iowa. A rebellious child, Gibbs was expelled from Catholic elementary school in sixth grade. Early in life, he began questioning the teachings of Catholicism and struggled to understand his relationship with God and the meaning of life. The information from two channeled entities, Seth and Abraham profoundly influences Gibbs. His research into Baha'ism, Buddhism, Christianity, Judaism, Hinduism,

Islam, Sufism and Taoism also greatly inform his spiritual and philosophical perspective. He incorporates quantum mechanics, physics and psychology as well as concepts from the works of Albert Einstein, Carl Jung, Sigmund Freud and Stephen Hawking.

Gibbs's communication style is concise, intense and deep. He would rather express wisdom in brief, powerful quotes and concise paragraphs rather than in complicated, long-winded explanations. Espresso Wisdom is short, strong, rich insight. Like espresso coffee, it gives an intense jolt of enlightenment. Enlightenment is an awakening, and Espresso Wisdom is meant to help jumpstart you on your journey.

Espresso Wisdom ☕
Short, Strong, Rich Insight! ™

Acknowledgments

IN THE SPIRIT OF *The Principle of Manifestation*, I wish to acknowledge the other aspects of myself and the collective consciousness for their ability to articulate profound wisdom in such a way that helped me understand and write this book. I express my gratitude to the following people and entities who have greatly inspired me along my path.

Jane Roberts and her series of channeled books entitled *Seth Speaks*, for showing me a wealth of profound information on the true nature of our reality.

Buddha, the founder of Buddhism, whose personal quest for enlightenment has illuminated my path with truth, wisdom and peace of mind. His succinct quotes are powerful, rich, insightful and completely accessible even today, thousands of years after his death.

Albert Einstein was one of the greatest minds in the history of mankind. His quotes speak to me with profound knowledge and clarity. I am in awe with his ability to articulate extremely complex concepts so simply.

Rumi, a Persian thirteenth-century poet and Sufi, so beautifully expressed wisdom that it is not surprising he is one of the most-read poets in the world. Some of Rumi's quotes are so incredibly simple yet so unbelievably deep that they have guided me toward effortless enlightenment.

Jesus Christ represents the emotional, devotional side of enlightenment for me. The Christian principles of love and forgiveness help to complete the wisdom of the circle of enlightenment.

Esther Hicks and her channeled material from the entity **Abraham** have provided me meaningful and practical information on the Principle of Manifestation.

Louise L. Hay is the quintessential guide for self-healing and physical-body manifestations. I continue to use her book ***You Can Heal Yourself*** as a guide to resolving any issues in my body.

Brian L. Weiss's book on reincarnation ***Many Lives, Many Masters*** opened my eyes to the multiple dimensions and lives of our existence. His work has shaped my understanding of the cycle of life and has provided a sense of peace and understanding that our existence is eternal.

Index of Quoted Authors

Louisa May Alcott (1832–1888) American novelist and poet best known for her novel *Little Women* and its sequels *Little Men* and *Jo's Boys*

Muhammad Ali (1942–2016) born **Cassius Marcellus Clay Jr,** American professional boxer and activist

James Allen (1864–1912) British philosopher, poet, inspirational author and a pioneer of the self-help movement best known for his work *As a Man Thinketh*

Aristotle (384 BC–322 BC) Greek philosopher, student of Plato; scientist and tutor of Alexander the Great; wrote on various subjects: physics, biology, zoology, metaphysics, logic, ethics, aesthetics, poetry, theater, music, rhetoric, linguistics, politics and government

Richard Bach (born 1936) American author best known for his books *Jonathan Livingston Seagull* and *Illusions: The Adventures of a Reluctant Messiah*

Roy T. Bennett (born 1957) American author of *The Light in the Heart*

Yogi Bhajan (1929–2004) born **Harbhajan Singh Puri**, legally changed his name to **Harbhajan Singh Khalsa** and also known as **Siri Singh Sahib** to his followers, Indian yogi, spiritual teacher, and entrepreneur

Helena Blavatsky (1831–1891) Russian occultist/esoteric philosopher, and author who co-founded the Theosophical Society in 1875

Claude M. Bristol (1891–1951) American journalist and author best known for his book *The Magic of Believing*

John K. Brown (born 1962) American author of Have *Faith in Love*

Les Brown (born 1945) American motivational speaker, author, radio DJ, former television host and former politician

Bill Bryson (born 1951) British-American author of books on travel, the English language, science and other nonfiction topics

Emma Bull (1954) American science fiction and fantasy author best known for her books *Bone Dance* and *War for the Oaks*

The Buddha, also known as Siddhartha Gautama (560 BC–477 BC); Born in what is now southern Nepal, he was the son of a king; he sought and achieved enlightenment

Rhonda Byrne (born 1945) Australian television writer and producer best known for her New Thought book and film *The Secret*

Pierre Teilhard de Chardin (1881–1955) French philosopher and Jesuit priest who conceived the idea of the Omega Point, a maximum level of complexity and consciousness to which he believed the universe is evolving

Deepak Chopra (born 1947) American author, public speaker, alternative-medicine advocate and a prominent figure in the New Age movement

Winston Churchill (1874–1965) British statesman, army officer, and writer, who served as Prime Minister of the United Kingdom from 1940 to 1945

Paulo Coelho (born 1947) Brazilian award-winning author of *The Alchemist*

Robert Collier (1885–1950) American author of self-help and New Thought metaphysical books whose work is referenced in the book and movie *The Secret*

Dalai Lama XIV (born Lhamo Dondrub in 1935) Tibetan Buddhist monk and spiritual and political leader of Tibet, living in exile in India

Walt Disney (1901–1966) American entrepreneur, animator, voice actor and film producer who was a pioneer of the American animation industry

Wayne Dyer (1940–2015) American self-help author, philosopher and motivational speaker

Meister Eckhart (1260–1327) born **Eckhart von Hochheim**. German theologian, philosopher and mystic

Albert Einstein (1879–1955) German-born physicist who developed the general theory of relativity and who is considered the most influential physicist of the twentieth century

John Elderidge (born 1960) American author, counselor, and lecturer on Christianity, known for his book *Wild at Heart*

Masaru Emoto (1943–2014) Japanese author, researcher, photographer and entrepreneur who claimed that human consciousness has an effect on the molecular structure of water

Mark Epstein (born 1953) American author and psychotherapist known for integrating both Buddha's and Sigmund Freud's approaches to trauma

Mahatma Gandhi (1869–1948) born **Mohandas Karamchand Gandhi,** Indian lawyer, politician, writer and activist leader of the Indian independence movement against British rule utilizing the practice of nonviolent civil disobedience

Seth Godin (born 1960) American entrepreneur and author best known for his books *Free Prize Inside*, *Purple Cow* and *The Dip*

Johann Wolfgang von Goethe (1749–1832) German poet, novelist, playwright, natural philosopher, diplomat, civil servant

Thích Nhất Hạnh (born 1926) Vietnamese Buddhist monk, teacher, poet, author and peace activist

Richard Conn Henry (born1940) American author and Professor of Physics and Astronomy at Johns Hopkins University

David Hewitt (born 1961) British attorney, author of *Focus: Best Ways to Improve Your Concentration and Improve Your Learning*

Esther Hicks (born 1948) American inspirational speaker and author best known for her work *The Law of Attraction* channeled from a group of non-physical entities called Abraham

Napoleon Hill (1883–1970) American journalist, salesman, lecturer and self-help author best known for his book *Think and Grow Rich*

T. F. Hodge (born 1969) American author, blogger, commentator and graphic designer known for his book *From Within I Rise*

Ernest Holmes (1887–1960) American New Thought writer, teacher, leader, author of *The Science of Mind* and founder of a Spiritual movement known as Religious Science

Karl Wilhelm von Humboldt (1767–1835) Prussian philosopher, linguist, government official, diplomat, and founder of the Humboldt University of Berlin

David Icke (born 1952) English writer, public speaker and former sports broadcaster and footballer, calling himself a "full time investigator into who and what is really controlling the world"

William James (1842–1910) American philosopher, psychologist, trained physician and the first educator to offer a psychology course in the United States

Sir James Jeans (1877–1946) English physicist, astronomer and mathematician

Jesus Christ (4 BC–AD 29) Born in Nazareth, known as the Son of God and the founder of the Christian religion, he was crucified for his teachings

Carl Jung (1875–1961) Swiss psychiatrist, psychoanalyst and founder of analytical psychology, best known for his psychological concepts of synchronicity, archetypal phenomena and the collective unconscious

Suzy Kassem (born 1975) American author, film director, philosopher, short story writer, essayist, and poet known for her book *Rise Up And Salute The Sun*

Søren Kierkegaard (1813–1955) Danish Christian philosopher and theologian who wrote critical texts on organized religion, Christianity, morality, ethics, psychology and philosophy of religion

Serge Kahili King (born 1954) American shaman, speaker and author of *Huna: Ancient Hawaiian Secrets for Modern Living*

Bruce Lee (1940–1973) American actor, martial artist, philosopher, filmmaker and founder of the martial art Jeet Kune Do

Michael Losier (born 1962) Canadian Law of Attraction trainer, teacher and author best known for his books *Law of Attraction*

David Lynch (born 1946) American filmmaker, painter, musician, actor, and photographer

Joyce Meyer (born 1943) born **Pauline Joyce Hutchison**, American Christian author and speaker and president of Joyce Meyer Ministries

Matt D. Miller (born 1976) American actor known for his work on Deja Vu, Big Fish and The Mechanic

Mary Manin Morrissey (born 1949) American New Thought minister, author, motivational speaker and co-founder of the Association for Global New Thought best known for her books *No Less Than Greatness and Building Your Field of Dreams*

Wolfgang Amadeus Mozart (1756–1791) German composer prolific in the classical era

Willie Nelson (born 1933) 1933) American musician, singer, songwriter, author, poet, actor, and activist

Sri Nisargadatta Maharaj (1897–1981) born **Maruti Shivrampant Kambli**, Indian Guru of nondualism belonging to the Inchagiri Sampradaya, a lineage of teachers from the Navnath Sampradaya and Lingayat Shaivism

Max Planck (1858–1947) German theoretical physicist whose discovery of energy quanta won him the 1918 Nobel Prize in Physics

Plato (428BC–348 BC) Greek philosopher, founder of the Academy in Athens; considered the central figure in the development of Western philosophy

Catherine Ponder (born 1927) American, Unity Church minster and inspirational author best known for her books *The Dynamic Laws of Prosperity* and *Millionaires of the Bible*

Bob Proctor (born1934) American author, business consultant, entrepreneur, life mentor and one of teachers of The Law of Attraction featured in *The Secret* book and movie

Ramana Maharshi (1879–1950) Born Venkataraman Iyer; Indian sage, guru and widely recognized enlightened being

Amit Ray (born 1960) Indian author and spiritual master, best known for his Om meditation, integrated yoga and Vipassana-meditation technique

James Redfield (born 1950) American author, lecturer, screenwriter and film producer best known for his book *The Celestine Prophecy*

Stephen Richards (born 1960) British author, film director and producer, clinical hypnotherapist, self-help expert

Sonia Ricotti (1901–1966) American author, motivational leader, radio host and entrepreneur best known for her books *Unsinkable: How to Bounce Back Quickly When Life Knocks You Down* and *The Law of Attraction Plain and Simple: Create the Extraordinary Life that You Deserve*

Anthony Robbins (born 1960) born **Anthony J. Mahavoric**, American author, entrepreneur, philanthropist and life coach known for his seminars, infomercials and self-help books *Unlimited Power* and *Awaken the Giant Within*

Franklin D. Roosevelt (1882–1945) American statesman and political leader who served as the President of the United States from 1933 to 1945

Rumi (1207–1273) Persian thirteenth-century poet and Sufi, Islamic scholar and theologian

Erwin Schrödinger (1887–1961) Austrian Nobel Prize-winning physicist for the formulation of the Schrödinger equation in quantum mechanics

Florence Scovel Shinn (1871–1940) American artist, book illustrator, New Thought spiritual teacher and metaphysical writer best known for her book *The Game of Life and How to Play It*

W. Clement Stone (1902–2002) American businessman, philanthropist and New Thought self-help book author best known for his book, coauthored with Napoleon Hill, *Success Through a Positive Mental Attitude*

Nikola Tesla (1856–1943) Serbian American inventor, electrical engineer, mechanical engineer, physicist and futurist best known for his contributions to the design of the modern alternating-current-electricity supply system

Henry David Thoreau (1817–1862) American essayist, poet, philosopher, abolitionist, naturalist, tax resister, development critic, surveyor, historian and transcendentalist best known for his book *Walden*

Eckhart Tolle (born 1948) German-born Canadian resident, spiritual teacher and author best known for his books *The Power of Now* and *A New Earth: Awakening to Your Life's Purpose*

Brian Tracy (born 1944) Canadian-American motivational public speaker and self-development author best known for his books *Earn What You're Really Worth*, *Eat That Frog!*, and *The Psychology of Achievement*.

Lao Tzu (605 BC–531 BC) Chinese philosopher, writer and presumed author of the Tao Te Ching

Leonardo da Vinci (1452–1519) Italian Renaissance polymath whose areas of expertise included painting, sculpting, architecture, science, music, mathematics, engineering, invention, literature, anatomy, geology, astronomy, botany, writing, history, and cartography

Joe Vitale (born 1952) American Law of Attraction author, coach, teacher, composer and actor best known for his contributions to the book *The Secret* and *The Secret* movie

Swami Vivekananda (1863–1902) Born Narendranath Datta; Indian Hindu monk, chief disciple of the Indian mystic Ramakrishna and a key figure in the introduction of the philosophies of Vedanta and Yoga to the Western world

Voltaire (1694–1778) pen name for **François-Marie Arouet,** French Enlightenment writer, historian and philosopher and advocate of freedom of religion, freedom of speech and separation of church and state

Andy Warhol (1928–1987) American painter, filmmaker, publisher, actor and major figure in the Pop Art movement

Wallace D. Wattles (1860–1911) American author and New Thought writer best known for his book *The Science of Getting Rich*

Marianne Williamson (born 1952) American spiritual teacher, author and lecturer who bases her teaching and writing on a set of books called *A Course in Miracles* channeled by Helen Schucman

Oprah Winfrey (born 1954) American media proprietor, talk-show host, actress, producer, and philanthropist best known for her talk show *The Oprah Winfrey Show*

Zig Ziglar (1926–2012) American author, salesman, and motivational speaker

www.ingramcontent.com/pod-product-compliance
Lightning Source LLC
LaVergne TN
LVHW050045090426
835510LV00043B/3094